VERNACULAR HISTORY SERIES

LIFE ON THE TRENT AND

Vernacular History Series

The 'Vernacular History' series of books and booklets, of which this is number one (although the second to be published) gives a picture of life 'as it really was'—or at least as it seemed to be to those living it at the time: and the time may be as early as the first decade of the twentieth century, or possibly even earlier, up to the quite recent past. There is no precise time of 'cut-off' and the intention of the series is to show life as it was experienced by those involved—and perhaps to correct impressions given by fictional events in a fictional landscape. The series is similar to the **Life in Lincolnshire** series except that the scene is not necessarily restricted to a Lincolnshire setting and titles may vary very considerably in length. The criterion for acceptance into the series is essentially personal experience. Polished literary expopsition may or may not be present—veracity is mandatory.

These accounts may sometimes be the work of men and women experienced in writing but also they may sometimes be the work of those who have not had the benefits of extended formal education and have never previously written for publication. So far as practicable editing has been kept to a minimum with the account being presented in the words of the author and any illustration being from contemporary material. Although memories are not infallible, and some recollected detail may have become embroidered with the passage of time, the books are intended as factual records of the experiences of men and women, in all social groups, which might not otherwise have been preserved.

No 1. — Life on the Trent and Humber Rivers

No 2. — All This and No Milk

A Tale of Life in the Holbeach Marshes - 1933-35

Life on The Trent and Humber Rivers

by

Arthur Caldicott

1970 1995

Richard Kay

80 Sleaford Road • Boston • Lincolnshire PE21 8EU

ISBN 0 902662 21 X

First published in December 1995
by Richard Kay Publications
80 Sleaford Road, Boston, Lincs. PE21 8EU
Telephone 01205 353231

Typeset by the publisher on an AppleMacintosh Plus computer using Microsoft Word and PageMaker applications. The main body of the text is set in Bookman 10 point type. The master copies were printed by means of an Apple LaserWriter Plus laser printer at 300 dpi.

Printed by
The Echo Press, Echo House, Jubilee Drive, Belton Park,
Loughborough, Leicestershire LE11 0XS

Contents

Illustrations

Illustration
Number Page.

Publisher's Note
and
Acknowledgements

The author of this small booklet sadly died shortly before the manuscript was submitted for publication. It has, consequently, not been possible to check and confirm some of the details given. Members of his family have helpfully provided details where possible but some facts remain unconfirmed although it is believed that the author's words have been accurately transcribed.

All the illustrations but one (a photograph of the *Hano*, – illustration No 4,) had been cut from newsprint or magazines. Despite extensive enquiries of all local papers in Hull, Grimsby, and Scunthorpe it has only proved possible to identify with certainty the origin of one—No 9, *Fort Fraser* aground—which appeared in the *Hull Daily Mail* and we are grateful both for their permission to publish and for them providing an actual photograph rather than, as in the majority of cases, having to reproduce from newsprint copies. The dates of some of the illustrations had been marked by the author but others may be uncertain. If we have inadvertently infringed copyright we shall be grateful if any copyright holder will contact us.

1. The sloop *Fanny* leaving Hull Hogwash. This is the boat owned by Ernest (Uncle) and Joseph William (Billie) Caldicott (Father) on which Arthur Caldicott first sailed and on which he was employed after his father had relinquished ownership and become a full-time pilot on the Humber and Trent Rivers.

1.

Memories of Early Days

I was born, in January 1916, in East Butterwick, a small village on the bank of the River Trent some four miles to the south-west of Scunthorpe, and my first introduction to the river, so I'm told, was when I fell into it at the age of three. Evidently I was standing on the bank with some of the other local children throwing stones into the fast-flowing water: I forgot to let go of mine and went in with it! I was rescued by means of a bucket tied onto the end of a clothes prop, and so began my long acquaintance with the river and its life.

My father and his brother owned a sloop which ran from Hull to several villages along the Trent, and from the early age of nine I was expected to help in this work. On a Sunday night my father would say: 'Look out for me on Wednesday at about three thirty to four o'clock'; and I had to make sure I was around the jetty ready to meet him. At around three, sure enough, I would see in the distance the Keadby Bridge (which had been opened in the year that I was born and had, by making road travel much easier, already affected the river traffic) raise and point to the sky, and then my Dad making his way back with the farmers' goods which formed his main cargo. Before reaching East Butterwick he would probably have called and delivered some stores at other Trent villages such as Burton-on-Stather, nearby May Dyke, Keadby and Burringham. My job was to help moor the ship by hanging the ropes onto the jetty, and offload the goods.

Some of the farmers would see him arrive and ask if he was going to "liver tonight', meaning to discharge the load. The decision was always his alone, so whether he said yes or no the farmers had to abide by it.

If he decided that he **would** unload that night, off would come the covers and hatches and I would go on board. Everything was done by hand in those days, and my job was to hang the sacks of cattle food, flour, maize etc. on to the hook which was then used to hoist them up on deck. There a man would heave each one up onto his back and stagger warily down the gantry with it to the bank. This was repeated until all was safe ashore, the time it took us to do it depending on the size of the particular cargo. When it was done, it was away home for a well-earned rest and a good meal.

In the morning at four or five o'clock my father would go out on his next call which was to West Butterwick, the village on the opposite bank of the river, where he would unload the rest of the goods to his customers on that side. As soon as the farmers saw him making his way across, they would begin to gather with their horses and carts ready to receive their goods. Then, if the tide was right, off he would go to Susworth, where the scene would be repeated, then on to Owston Ferry where the last load would be delivered. When he arrived home he would usually do a little maintenance work on the boat ready for the next tide.

It was the tides which dictated all his movements, of course, so sometimes he would set off on the next trip during the Sunday night, sometimes it would be Monday morning. He always told my mother what time he expected to be home, and he was never late, which gives a fair indication of his experience of the river and its times, and his knowledge of the winds by which he sailed.

During the twenties this river was relatively as busy as the M 62 is now, and there were hundreds of barges, keels, and sloops making use of it. The United Towing Company alone had ten or twelve tugs working the river, and I knew every single boat. As soon as we spotted one of them coming around the bend we would guess its name, and there have been times when I've seen as many as seven of them all making their way along within half a mile of each other. On rare occasions we would see one of these tugs sailing upstream, 'punching the tide' as we called it, and it was fascinating to watch it making its way laboriously against the natural flow of the river. It was considered an unusual event because the normal practice for these boats was to make good use of the currents to get where they wanted to go. Then when the tide was 'played out' and would no longer carry them it was common to see one of the bargees, such as my father, go out and drop anchor so the tug could tie up alongside him, and there they would stay until the tide changed.

2. In days, perhaps a decade, before the Second World War there was a regular paddle steamer service between Hull and Gainsborough which called at most villages between. Improved roads and vehicles rendered this form of transport obsolete; initially for passengers and soon also for 'goods'.

There were also some little boats used to ferry people to and from their ships anchored up in the middle of the river. They were a kind of rowing boat with a keep and one oar used astern, and I learned to scull one of these dinghies when I was eight or nine years old. I would hang the 'painter' onto a bollard on board the ship, and then let the boat drift out as far as it would go, which was a distance of about fifteen to twenty feet. From there I would scull my way back again, which was an excellent method for a novice to learn to handle a boat, as one had plenty of practice yet could do it virtually in complete safety. I used to repeat this ritual over and over again, longing all the time for the day when my father would give me permission to scull the boat alone across the river. Then the happy day arrived, although it wasn't altogether as easy as I had thought it would be.

It was a frosty winter's morning and my father had to pick someone up from the other side of the river. He asked me if I thought I could make it across from East Butterwick to West Butterwick. Of course I said I was sure I could manage it, so he decided to let me have a go.

Within minutes I was sculling proudly across the ice-cold water of a river whose reputation was one of dangerous tides and treacherous cross-currents which required the lifelong experience of the 'bargee' to handle. In fact the danger, when it came, was from a totally different direction to the one I had expected.

I was about halfway across the river when a tug came running light (i.e. not towing a boat) and I watched in terror as it headed straight for me. I stood up in the dinghy, which was a very dangerous thing to do midstream, and held my arms outstretched in the wild hope of pushing myself out if its path. Somehow luck was with me, as it swept past without actually doing me any damage at all, although I did lose direction for a few minutes. Feeling rather shaken, I continued across, hoping everything was now going to be alright, but developed another problem of a different nature altogether; my bare hands became raw in the icy air, and by the time I reached the other side I was sobbing with the pain.

The passenger I had gone to collect was going to take the job of mate aboard my father's ship, and he alternately soothed me and called me 'a big bab' as he sculled the boat back across to the other side. It didn't take long, however, before I got used to it all, and soon I was an expert, as was fitting for the son of a bargee.

About two years after that, my father took me with him on one of his trips, which I thought was absolutely wonderful. This was to be my very first taste of the River Humber, and I found it a marvellous river, full of excitement. I used to go on these trips whenever I had any school holidays, and it was after I'd been on the third or fourth that I discovered that there was an island in the middle of the river called 'Read's Island'. There was even a farm on it, with several people living there, and it was used for grazing cattle as the grass there was very good.

From Burton Stather to Gainsborough the name of Caldicott was well known on the river, especially my father's, which was Billy, and everyone knew our family, as well as our sloop. The river was a very friendly place, where you could always find friends at every mooring spot, waving and shouting greetings from along the banks as we passed.

People knew everything that happened on the river, and were quick to pass on news whether good or bad. During my schooldays a notable incident on the river was the accidental sinking of a small barge loaded with flour from the firm of Joseph Rank and Co. The barge was named *As You Like It*, and after it had been under water for a couple of days it must have rolled over, releasing its cargo of flour in ten stone sacks. People lining the banks, up and down the river, will remember the sight of scores of sacks bobbing up and down, and it wasn't long before they sculled out to get them. The flour was so fine that the water only penetrated two or three inches into it, so most of the contents remained undamaged and provided a free supply of flour for weeks for those quick enough to get them into their pantries!

There were jetties for loading and unloading goods at Keadby, Burringham, East and West Butterwick, Susworth, and Owston Ferry. They were always called 'landings' by those who used them and were in constant use during the time when the steam packet sailed from Hull to Gainsborough. All these jetties were built the same way, and the one I remember best was at Burton Stather. They each had two fixed decks, one either side of the central deck which was secured to the bank itself, but which was movable, so that whatever the height of the tide when the packet arrived, the winches could lift up the deck to the ship's level, ensuring that the passengers could get ashore easily. In my father's day, they were still in operation, although even then they were beginning to fall into a state of disrepair, once the steamship had stopped running. By the thirties, as trade on the river dropped and no-one used them any more, they gradually disappeared altogether.

It was at about this time that the 'Rank's and Goole Tillage Company' got their first lorries, and this was to have a major effect on the river and its trade, principally because of the question of speed. Once it became established, all that the farmers had to do was to ring up with their orders and the goods were delivered by the next day, which was, of course, far quicker than the three or four days it took for someone like my father to bring them. This innovation was eventually to cost him his business.

He decided to sell the boat in favour of a job as a pilot, which paid much better money, but for a time, did both jobs together. As trade increased, he engaged other men to supervise the barge trips so that he could keep up with the piloting job, and I well remember the men he employed. These included Arthur Leaman, Albert Smith, Charlie Houghton and Albert Gilliat, who was my favourite as he did everything at the double, being a very fit man—you had to be pretty fit, of course, to be able to do the job at all!

My father continued to employ men for some time, but the coasters didn't pass often enough at that time for him to be able to earn a living by it. He gradually realised that he wasn't bringing in enough to clear his expenses, or, as he used to put it, the profit was about the price of a quarter of tea.

He first became a pilot in 1925, and remained one until he retired at the age of seventy.

• • 0 • •

As he was a mariner using the river regularly, my father received a 'log' every month which was produced by the river authorities, and which gave an up-to-date description of the positions of the buoys and lightships in the channel. This was very important as the pattern of sandbars and shallows changed frequently, and it was extremely easy to run aground if you didn't navigate with care. I used to study these logs closely, as it was my ambition to be able to navigate the river like my father, and it wasn't long before I got the hang of it. Nevertheless, as I had always been taught, I always treated the river with respect, especially as the Humber during a strong tide or wind can get very rough indeed.

On one occasion I was at my aunt's house when a letter arrived which was 'written backwards'. (This was a frequent ploy used by adults who didn't want the children to be able to read what was written in them: to decipher them all you had to do was to hold them up to the mirror.) It was from my uncle, who often worked with my father on the trips, and said simply: 'Sorry to tell you we have blown the mast out and are in Barton dry dock.' The mast had been broken off by the strong winds and had snapped just above the hatches. To repair it they had to cut out the eight or so feet of it that were left in the hold of the ship, and reshape the rest of it so it could be replaced. The only difference this seemed to make to the boat was to reduce her speed a bit.

Life on the river was certainly not all plain sailing, as on another occasion they 'stemmed' a trawler (collided with it), costing them some new beams.

Although I had already begun to make the acquaintance of the river, it was only when I sailed in my own boat that I truly began to understand it.

My brother had given me a dinghy, complete with mast, sail and oars, and I spent all my spare time out on the river with my salmon net and twelve bore shotgun. I had soon explored every 'bight' sandbank in the river and I loved every minute of it. I used to think nothing of rowing as far as Whitton Ness on the Trent just to look for salmon, and it was while I was at that spot that I first saw the 'Eagre' or 'Bore' as people call it.

The Eagre is the name given to the wave which comes down the river at certain times of the year, and here it was about four or five inches high, although it would be about three feet high by the time it reached Butterwick, and nearer six feet at Owston Ferry.

These, then, were my early experiences on the rivers.

2.

Moving On

I can remember three ferrymen operating on the river. There was Rol Readhead crossing from Burton Stather to Garthorpe; Harry Smith crossing from West to East Butterwick; and Ike Petit at Owston Ferry. Their services gradually died away, as did others on the river, and it's a shame, in my opinion, because they could tell you a thing or two, being very experienced men who rowed their own boats and kept them in immaculate condition.

There was a village pump on the river bank, which was serviced by a man called Dick Coy. If he had any repairs to do he used to go to people's houses and collect one penny from each to cover the cost. At that time many people drank the water from the Trent, as I did myself for fifteen years. It was taken from the river on neap* tides, and I used to carry two bucket loads to a dolly tub at the house. (If I helped by collecting it for other people who might ask me, I could earn two or three pennies at a time.) We used to let the water stand for a day or so, until the mud settled down to the bottom of the tub. After that, you could take a glassful, and it would be as clear as gin. When we moved into a house with a well it was a wonderful thing, we thought, to have water all the year round, and it seemed miraculous later on when we got water laid on properly, and had electricity as well.

In about 1929 we moved house and went to live at West Butterwick on the opposite side of the river. It was about two

---

* A neap tide is a tide of minimum amplitude when the sun and the moon are operating against each other. This is when there has probably been the least movement of the water and consequently likely to be the time when there is the least sediment stirred up in the water.

years after this that my father sold the sloop (which incidentally was called *Fanny*). Everybody knew this ship, and it was sold to a man called Tom Abbey, a very daring but in my opinion not very experienced sailor, as I was later to discover.

Tom hadn't had the ship long when he approached me to ask if I'd like to join him as his mate. I reminded him that he already had a mate, but he said that he wasn't any good, and that he would prefer me to help him, so I made arrangements to join him at Hull the following weekend. This was to be the first of many trips I was to make, and I shall never forget it.

When he met me on the pier he took me to the ship, which was laid up in what they called 'the creek', a narrow strip of mooring space running between Albert Dock and Humber Dock. He told me that we were going up to the river Hull on which the city of Hull is built, to load slaughter house manure. I knew that this would mean 'launching' (pushing the ship along by means of boathooks) which was usually done when you didn't have power or couldn't use it if you had it.

We finally got it all loaded up, and set off, but the ship wouldn't steer properly. The reason for this was that he had put all the manure in the front of the boat, and it was far heavier than the lighter stuff he had decided to put aft. The boat was now sailing three inches 'by the head', meaning that it was tilted downward at a dangerous angle in the water, and was very unstable. We were very fortunate to be helped a little by the *Greendale* which gave us a tow back to the pier.

The *Greendale* was a great ship which travelled up the river weekly, and even if you couldn't see her you could always tell when she was going by because of the distinctive sound of her exhaust. A strange coincidence was that one day during the war, I had to go to the War Office and the following day to Teddington Laboratory, where I saw a photo of her. I deduced from this that she must have been 'modelled' there.

Once tied up at the pier, Tom went to get us some food, and when he returned I pointed out that 'the ball was up'.

The 'ball' was a metal ball about two foot six in diameter which was wound up so that everyone in the harbour mouth could see it and judge just how windy conditions were.

Despite the poor outlook, Tom gave the order to hoist up the mainsail and get going, and as he was the skipper, I had no option but to do as I was told. I knew that my father would never have dreamt of going out with such a load in those conditions, but the skipper lacked the experience to know better, so off we went, out into the Humber, without even hatches and covers over the hold.

We set off for New Holland tacking all the way because of the strong Westerly wind. My job was to lash the foresail to the rigging as we tacked one way, then when we turned, to let it go so that we would travel forward in the right direction. As soon as one movement was completed, I would prepare for the next tack. The unpleasant part of it was that as the hold was open to the elements, I had to jump into the manure at each turn to avoid the wash which was coming over the bows of the boat. The problem was that all the water was going into the manure, which added to the weight in a boat that was already 'three inches by the head'. The result of all this was that we couldn't make any headway at all, try as we might, and it took us more than three hours of hard labour before Tom would admit that it was hopeless.

He ordered me to drop anchor near Hessle. I then made my way aft, where to my horror I discovered that the cabin was awash with the water we had taken on board. My shoes, the stool, the carpets, everything in fact was submerged to a depth of about two feet.

It was at times like this that you realised the difficulties of the days before mechanisation; we had to get the hand pumps out and start working like fury to get rid of the excess water. We were at it for hours and hours, but when day broke we saw something that made us realise just how lucky we'd been, especially considering the weather of the previous night.

About five hundred yards from our position, we could see

what looked like the funnel and masts of a ship, although it wasn't until two days later that we found out it was the *Edgar Wallace*, a trawler which had dragged her anchor, hit a sandbank and turned over. Only two or three of the crew had been picked up after the accident. I think that this was probably the most frightening moment I ever experienced on the rivers.

Tom and I stayed anchored off Hessle for one set of tides, then made our way to the Trent on the following tide. It took us another tide to get to West Butterwick and yet another to reach Gunthorpe, our destination, which made it five tides in all. A good skipper would have been able to do the whole trip in only one tide, so you can now understand what I meant when I said it was a question of experience.

When we arrived at our destination and it was time for the cargo to be unloaded, I was the one who had the unenviable task of heaving all the manure out of the hold. It was then put onto barrows and wheeled away. As soon as the job was completed, the farmer gave everyone twenty-six shillings each, which in my case went straight to my boss, and from which I was paid twenty-four (a good wage in those days).

Two days after the *Edgar Wallace* accident, we were in Butterwick enjoying a cup of tea at my mother's when my father suddenly arrived. Of course we told him all about the incident, thinking it would be news to him to hear our story. We were thunderstruck to discover that he had seen us 'laid off Hessle', and even more staggered to find that he had almost run into us during that eventful night!

One of the Everards' coasters, the *Angularity*, had been passing as the *Edgar Wallace* got into difficulty, and my father had been the one piloting it. He had heard cries for help from the area around the ship and went to its aid, but was unable to find more than one survivor in the water. It was as he went to pick him up that he narrowly avoided running into our sloop in the darkness.

We heard that as the crew were trying to raise the *Edgar Wallace* they had positioned a wreck-lifting ship on one side of her. There was a tug from the 'United Towing Company' on the other side, and together they had placed hawsers under the ship in order to hoist her up out of the water by means of winches on the bigger ship. Unfortunately, as they began winching, the tug which was taking the weight of the ship coming up through the water turned over. It was obviously too small to handle the operation. This had cost another life, as Jim Vessey, the oldest man in the fleet at the time, was drowned. In the end only two or three of the crew were ever rescued, which is one reason why I have said that it was a hard life on the rivers in those days.

There's no doubt that the outward trip had been eventful, but the return journey was to be even more so!

We set off from Gunthorpe 'under the foresail', meaning that we didn't use full sail as the weather was still very rough. As we approached Keadby Bridge, we sounded the foghorn as that was the procedure for notifying the bridge operators that we wanted to go through it. As was often the case, we had to wait as a train was due to go over the bridge, so we rounded up, dropped anchor and listened for the bell which was the signal that all was clear.

Once past the bridge, the skipper decided that he wanted to travel as fast as possible to get as far down the river as we could before the tide turned, so he hoisted the mainsail with a couple of reefs in it to shorten it. We then went belting along until we came to the junction of the Trent, Humber and Ouse at a place called East Trent, where we met with disaster.

A wall was being put up at this place, and there were piles driven deep into the river bed and banked with stones. Unfortunately, we got a bit too close to it, and rammed straight into it with all the force of the four horse power engine on board. The dinghy was immediately holed and we were forced to lower all the sails to prise the boat off the wall. If that wasn't bad enough, we had no sooner got under way again than the skipper told me that the dingy had filled with water and that we would have to run her aground to do immediate repairs.

We got the main halyards hung onto the dinghy and began to heave the boat out of the water. The halyards broke. We found another set and rigged it so that I could heave the skipper up to the mainsail pulley in the hope that he would be able to thread the new halyard through the top pulley. At that moment a snowstorm blew up and began to buffet the boat. I looked up to see Tom swinging in the chair with the snow whipping round his 'long johns', and although it was a terrible thing for a man to be up there in those conditions, I couldn't help but laugh at the sight he looked.

We finally managed to get it up, hitched up the dinghy in a safe position, and stayed put until the next ebb tide. We continued our journey using the foresail only as the gale was still blowing. By the time we reached Hull it was nearly dark, and Tom turned the boat into the dock at a very daring speed, being, as I have said, a bold sort of a man. He then turned into the creek and went straight up onto the mudbank which had built up over the years. He jumped ashore, hung a 'head rope' on, said 'Goodnight, see you in the morning', and went home, leaving me on board alone for the night.

When I got up the following morning, the rope had broken, and the boat had slipped off the mud, so there I was, afloat in the basin! I used a boathook and brute force, and managed to get the boat back to the quayside. I made sure this time that she was tied up good and tight, after which I sat down to wait for the skipper to reappear.

This was only one of hundreds of trips that I made, and I have described it in some detail just to give an idea of what it was really like in those days – a lot of mighty hard work!

3.

Changing Times

There were a lot of innovations on the rivers during the thirties, one example of which was the decision to build a wall at the Trent End in an attempt to save the banks, which were being washed away very quickly. They began by driving wooden piles into the banks of the Trent and the Ouse along a distance of about half a mile, then dropping thousands of tons of slag lumps around them. This was done in sections, as I recall. During high tide some parts of the wall were above the water-line while others were submerged, and there was a pylon with half a dozen lights on it to warn mariners that it was there. Even so, navigation from the Humber into the Trent wasn't difficult except in bad weather. The only real danger was that the tides were very fast and had formed a sandbank or 'bar' across the 'V' shaped entrance to the Trent.

I remember seeing the boat of one pilot who must have got lost, and who had run into the partly-finished wall, then tried to come back off it. As he attempted to do this, he had struck a part of the wall which was higher than the place where he had gone in and he had caught fast on the slag rocks. When we sailed past, what caught our eye was a number of red lights halfway down the wall. We wondered what on earth it could be, as it was unusual to see red lights at a place where there weren't any mooring spots or marked hazards. When we approached, we could see the stem of his boat raised four or five feet out of the water.

In the end the boat simply slipped off the wall with the lowering of the water level at low tide, and continued on her way to Hull. There she was inspected and given twenty-seven new plates before the authorities would allow her to sail out of the Humber.

Around this time I recall another incident. I was sailing up river early one morning when we noticed a small coaster sitting high and dry in a grass field about seventy to a hundred yards from the water. The ship was called the *River Witham*, and it had lost its way during a foggy night at a time when the spring tide had run over the banks and into the field beyond. Having strayed into the field it was stranded there for six weeks as they waited for each tide to lift them so that they could get back into the river. In the end the army used Fire Service pumps, so I'm told, to wash the soil away in front of her so that she could slip gradually back into the river. Of course there was no radar in those days and the skipper went up the river without a pilot, hoping to get away with it. They were lucky that the ship wasn't damaged.

Most of the barges, keels, and sloops towed a small boat or dinghy which was used mainly in emergencies. For instance, if they 'ran out of tide' and had to wait for the next one before they could continue their journey, they had to anchor for twelve hours or so. They would then use their dinghy to get rations and suchlike to last them during their stay. Also, if they overran their destination, they would take a rope to the shore using the dinghy, fix the rope securely and return to the ship where they would begin heaving on the windlass to winch the ship back to where they should be. This was exhaustingly hard work as they had only manpower to achieve this. We had to use brute force for everything in those days, but we managed somehow.

Another tragedy which occurred in the Humber was when two trawlers, the *Delphine* and the *Lady Jeannette*, collided in the river opposite the 'Alexandra Dock'. The tide carried the crippled *Lady Jeannette* upstream, and although she blew her horn to ask for help as soon as she hit a sandbank, she sank within seconds. I heard that nine men were lost, and nine rescued. A German lifting ship was hired to raise her, but it was called home rather abruptly before it could do so, as the

3. The *Lady Jeanette* being raised using a steel-hawser 'cradle', which had been passed beneath her, between two salvage vessels.

war was about to break out at that time. It was to be quite some time before the *Jeannette* was lifted.

The two rivers both deserve their reputations as being treacherous, the Humber because of her sandbanks, and the Trent for the deceptive speed of the tides.

The spring tides are very fast, reaching speeds of up to nine knots per hour. (In normal circumstances the Trent 'fills up' as we say in about five hours. During spring tides I've seen her fill up in under four hours.)

The tide changes on average every twelve hours and twenty minutes, and their depths are officially gauged at the Albert dock 'sill' in Hull.

A name for a tide commonly heard on the rivers was a 'blown tide'. The tide normally comes in from the east through the River Humber. On a spring tide, if the wind is in the west, the tide is held in check on the lea side of the country and is blown back into the Humber, which causes a rise of three feet or more on the normal level of the water. This naturally causes flooding, especially in the lower areas of the city of Hull itself, and creates a dreadful mess with the deposit of four to six inches of mud at each of these 'blown tides'. As boys, we loved to see the river so full, and we gloated over the extra areas covered by water, but, of course, it was a different and sadder story for those whose homes were devastated.

During the Thirties, the steelworks firm of John Lysaghts built a wharf at Flixborough which received the largest steamship ever to come up the Trent; she was a Swedish ship called the *Hano*. She was piloted by my father, and was assisted by a tug called the *Welshman*. The ship was loaded with foreign ore and was emptied of this cargo by means of an electric crane and grabs.

There was a regular flow of coasters at this time for what was known as the 'coal drops'. They stopped at Keadby Wharf, and I've seen as many as thirteen waiting there for their consignment of coal. All these ships had to have a pilot as they were necessary for insurance purposes, especially since this area was so busy. (There were three pilots working on the Trent until the war broke out).

4. The Swedish ship *Hano* assisted by the tug *Welshman.* Thought by Joseph William (Billy) Caldicott, the author's father, who piloted her, to be the largest ship ever to enter the Trent.

In 1938 they held the last regatta at Owston Ferry.

This was a great day for anyone who loved boats, as there were dinghies all along the river Trent. There were three from Keadby, two from West Butterwick, and many more from the other side of Owston Ferry. We arrived in time for the sailing race which was due to commence at twelve o'clock with the high water. A man called Belly Leggott won it for the simple reason that he had more canvas than a Big Top, as we used to say, and although there wasn't much wind that day he got all the benefit of what there was with those sails! My own brother, Ernest, came in second, and he also won the rowing race.

The money for the prizes came from a collection taken from the spectators on the banks, and, as there was usually a huge crowd, this often amounted to a lot of cash.

Another event that was very popular was the blindfold sculling, in which the contestants had to put a paper bag over their heads and scull across the river by instinct and sheer skill. I can assure you that it isn't nearly as easy as it sounds to cross a river in a straight line.

I was very lucky as I got the feel of the current quite quickly, and I pulled steadily across as fast as I dared. The trouble was that I had no way of telling how well I was doing or who might be beating me. All I knew was that right from the start there was complete and utter pandemonium going on all around me. I could hear boats running into one another, boatmen swearing like troopers, and all the while the people on the banks laughing fit to bust.

It took all my concentration to get across, and no-one was more surprised than I was when I got there and was informed by the officials that I had won the contest!

When I took off the blindfold and turned round, I saw the reason for all the laughing. Some of the boats were facing the wrong direction, some hadn't even managed to get away from the bank, and some couldn't keep a straight course so they were miles downriver, still going hell for leather! (These were eventually towed back by a motor boat which was standing by for exactly that purpose.)

There was a barge anchored in the channel, and its hold contained cases upon cases of IPA (Indian Pale Ale) and Anchor beer, as well as heaps of delicious ham sandwiches.

A 'greasy pole' had also been set up on this barge, and we were told that the man who succeeded in walking along it and then managed to remove the flag on the end of it would win a whole ham, as was the custom.

I had my eye on the other traditional contest - the pillow fight on a pole - and eventually came out the winner. What with the prize from that and the cash I won for the sculling (£3. 0s. 0d or £4. 0s. 0d.) I considered it wasn't a bad day's work for an August Bank Holiday!

This used to be an annual event, but, as I said, it was the last one ever held as the war put a stop to this and to many more of our peace-time pleasures and they were not restarted in the changed conditions of the post war times.

4.

The War and Beyond

The outbreak of the war put a stop to almost everything on the Trent, as very few of the foreign coasters came up after that, and the number of smaller trade ships also dropped.

My father went to sea on one of Mitchell's ships, the *Daniel M.* He was injured after some time, and worked in a rope factory at Hull, but as soon as ever he could manage it, he went back to the job he knew best – piloting the rivers.

By that time I had moved on into Scunthorpe to work at the steelworks, but I kept in touch with what was going on along the river, mainly through my father, but also through the voluntary work I was doing for the 'Trent River Patrol'.

The patrol had depots at Burton Stather and Owston Ferry, but their headquarters were at Keadby. Their work was similar to that of the Home Guard, and they had two boats at their disposal to carry out their duties.

We used to have evening meetings, and at the weekends we would go on manoeuvres. One week, for instance, we would 'attack' Burton, and another time it would be Owston Ferry. We all took the whole thing very seriously, and felt it was very good experience should Hitler ever decide to try and take our river!

I did these jobs until I was called up. During the time I was waiting to go into the Army, none of us ever went hungry as I still had my boat, gun, and salmon net, as well as being able to hunt rabbits, hares and birds. All it needed was a bit of nerve and a certain amount of skill. Once I left for the Army, my father moved to Hull, as this made it easier for him in his work as a pilot.

After the Dunkirk evacuation, we had the West Kent

Regiment stationed in the area, and three of their sergeants lodged with us for a while. They were really great lads, and we thought a lot of them.

One day, they decided that they wanted to borrow my dinghy—to go out on the river for pleasure, they said. I explained to them that the only pleasure you could really gain from sailing like that on the river was to travel up and down it according to the tide, as the currents were far too strong for anyone otherwise to row comfortably. They weren't convinced by this, and said they still wanted to go out in it there and then. I had very strong doubts about the wisdom of the whole escapade, but they were a long way from home and I felt sorry for them, so in the end I let them go. I was working my shift at the steelworks when they returned two hours later, so it was some time before I discovered just how disastrous that decision had been.

They had completely broken one of the oars, and had obviously lost another somewhere along the way, which meant they must have really been pushing it to limp home on the remaining two. I was very angry and disappointed about the whole thing, not only because I had already warned them of the dangers, but also because they hadn't told me about the damage, and had just left me to find out for myself. The episode taught me a lesson about following one's instincts!

The war affected us very little in terms of bombing, and, although we had a few incendiary bombs, the only place on the Trent that was seriously attacked, as far as I can remember, was the Nitro Fertilizer plant at Flixborough.

In about 1945, things seemed to prosper a bit more around the rivers: factories were set up in the Humber mouth, and Immingham dock flourished as work came in from all directions.

I have records of my father's work as a pilot which state that he had thirty-four ships in one month—more than one each day—which means that he boarded them, and took each one from Hull to Keadby or vice versa. He would get on the tide early and, if the ship was light (unladen) and could go full steam all the way, he would reckon on maybe two more hours of flow, so he could set off back on his next trip. He used to do this two or three times a month, which shows how busy the pilots must have been.

In those days, most ships were 'lighters', and their cargo was mainly coal. Many, many thousands of tons of it were unloaded at Keadby and taken from there all round the country. At Flixborough, coasters brought thousands of tons of foreign ore, and dozens of lighters brought coking ore from the Yorkshire pits. Some of these used the river Ouse, but the majority used the Keadby and South Yorkshire canal. Most of the lighters got two trips a week, and some of them got three, although those were privately owned. All these materials were transported by rail to the B.S.C. steel works (British Steel Corporation), who owned the railway which was built at the same time as the jetty.

I spent four years at the steelworks and it was my job to run the coal and the iron ore up to the steelworks, so I was always in contact with the river. In fact, because almost everyone knew my father, the men were always telling me stories about what he was up to!

One of these was about a time when they were loading one of the Lysaght's ships, and my father was on board earlier than he actually needed to be as they were still loading. The traffic manager from the works was there, witnessing the loading, when my father said that the load they had got on was all that they should take. The manager insisted that they should do just one more, at which my father calmly said that if they did one more 'slingful' he wouldn't go. The manager still ordered one slingfull more. He then told my father he was going to have to sail. 'Not until the morning we won't', replied my father, totally unmoved, and they didn't. My father knew what he was talking about, as, if he had set off late he might have missed the tide and gone aground somewhere, which would have meant a twelve hour wait before they could have got going again. The manager was furious, but after that confrontation he never again attempted to interfere with my father's decisions!

When the pilots received news that there was a ship due, one of the first questions asked was what draught she had as, of course, that affected the navigation. It was unusual to see ships of a great size coming up the river and on occasions when a particularly big ship did come up we were all interested in seeing her make her way along.

One Sunday I heard that there was a ship called the *Gallium* due to come up the river that evening, so my wife, son, and I cycled over to watch it. When they moored the ship to the jetty, I had a chat with Harry, who told me that my father had done a marvellous job of navigation that day. They were drawing seventeen feet ten inches of water (which means that the boat needed at least that depth of water to be able to pass), yet there were only seventeen feet nine inches available at the mouth of the Trent, due to the sandbar situated there. I don't need to go into the reasons why they needed the tug to take them through!

In fact, my father maintained that during his time there had never been a ship that came into the river Trent that drew eighteen feet or more, and although this may provoke some disagreement, I take his word for it.

Many of the ships used to go up to Goole and transfer some of their cargo into barges to lessen the draught so that it would only amount to ten to twelve feet.

Just after the war, the J. Wharton Shipping Company built a wharf at Gunness, which is now know as Gunness Grove. Ironstone Wharf was sold to Eccles Slag Company, and both of these became very busy. Gunness had five berths and handled all kinds of materials, while Eccles had three berths. Many of the Wharton ships were named after their family, e.g. the *Jackonia*, the *Brendonia*, the *Stevonia* and so on. Taking the

5. The *Gallium* unloading iron ore at Flixborough in February 1955 *en route* for John Lysaght's works in Scunthorpe. As she drew 17' 10" and there were only 17' 9" of clearance at the mouth of the Trent it needed precise navigation, good seamanship and perhaps a little luck to get her into the Trent. Once unloaded of course there would have been no problem in getting her out of the Trent into the Humber again.

6. A German 'prize ship' in Hull in June 1945. Probably the first German ship to arrive since the war (which had ended in Europe only in May). The ship, the *Mittel Meer,* discharging her cargo of sugar beet and molasses at Saltend had been brought by a German crew who had returned to Germany after handing over to a British crew. The ship was still fitted with anti-aircraft guns and minesweeping equipment.

7. The *Stevonia* being launched on a foggy day at Selby.

Stevonia as an example, it weighed 2,415 tonnes, cost what was then a staggering £2.5 million, and was launched at the Selby shipyard of Cochrane Shipbuilders. At the owner's request it was built of British steel mainly from the British Steel Corporation at Scunthorpe. It measured 79 metres (259 feet) in length. with a draught of 4.55 metres (14 feet 11 inches). It was a multi-purpose cargo vessel and with a main engine power of 999 bhp it could make 10.5 knots (which in landlubber's terms is almost 12 miles per hour). As the picture shows it had been launched late in 1985 in thick fog in the spectacular sideways manner onto the River Ouse and completed in the following year. The launch ceremony was performed by Mrs Wharton, the mother of managing director

Steve Wharton, after whom the vessel was named. They also had a coaster called the *Trentonia* and two or three others. They handled all kinds of materials and used the old coal drop jetties at Keadby. Some of these jetties are now obsolete, and many of them are not very busy now.

There were also pumping stations all along the rivers, and these were run by steam. All the coal was delivered by lighters, which were barges used especially for this purpose. Extra men would be engaged to discharge the coal, and it was all done by hand, which was extremely hard work! Nowadays, these pumps have, of course, been converted to run by motor, and their fuel is brought by tanker, which is a lot easier and cleaner. Some of them are now also run by electricity.

8. A barge approaching the Keadby Bridge without the need to raise the bridge to allow passage.

Of all the many people I met on the rivers, two men in particular stand out in my mind as memorable characters, typical of the kind of folk who lived and worked there.

One was called Bill Crampton, and he used to catch eels. He made the traps himself out of willow twigs cut from the trees along the banks. He would weave these into baskets, and set his 'leaps', as he called them, down onto the bed of the river. Once they were in place under the water, no-one else could ever find them, although Bill himself knew exactly where they were. I used to wish with all my heart that I had the secret of his marking system! Many and many a time did I spy on him as he was setting his traps, and as soon as I saw him leave, I would tear down to my boat and head for the exact spot where I was sure he had been, but never once did I find them.

Bill lived at Susworth, and the day after I had seen him go out on the river, he would call round the houses, his bicycle loaded down with freshly-caught eels, and rabbits, which was another of his side-lines. The price in those days was one shilling and sixpence for a rabbit, and ninepence for a pound of eels, and Bill would stand there and skin whatever you bought from him. He never carried any scales with him, but the weight was right or, if not precise, erred on the generous side.

When he had sold all he could in our village, he would climb back on his bike, a famous sight as it had the most enormously thick wheels, and off he would go to the next place. That bike carried as many as a hundred rabbits, and over four stones of eels, but I never saw him bring any unwanted stuff back, so he must have been a very popular trader.

There aren't many people who eat eels these days, but I used to love them. When I really fancied some, I used to go 'blobbing', which is what we called it when we went fishing for eels. It used to take me two days to get everything set up for it. First of all I'd wait until the evening when I'd flood the pavement outside the house with water. Worms of all sizes would soon come up and I could gather them up without any trouble. The following day, I'd get a metal spoke from an old umbrella, my 'bodkin' as it was known, and I'd thread my worms onto a piece of worsted until I had a lovely big fat bunch of them hanging there. These would usually keep for two or three days before going off.

My weight was a cornet-shaped lump of lead, and this would go on the line fastened to a good long stick. To store the eels once caught, I used to tack an old sack onto the stem of my dinghy, and I'd wet it well so that it hung, drooping a bit towards the middle. That is where I would make a hole, and underneath this funnel-shaped net I would set a good solid bucket. Now I was ready to go out on the ebbing tide to catch my eels.

I had my own favourite places to go 'blobbing', and I would lower the worsted with the eels on. As they snapped at the bait, the worsted would get caught on their teeth, and I could haul them up, sometimes as many as four or five in one go if they were biting well that day. It took some doing to get them hauled in because they weighed several pounds each, but once I had them in the dinghy all I had to do was to shake them over the sack spread out at the end of the boat. Off they would fall, wriggling about until they ended up dropping through the hole in the centre and down into the bucket.

I've always classed myself an expert with eels, as I could skin them as fast as they were passed to me. I just wish that there had been deep freezers in those days—then I could have enjoyed eels all the year round!

The other man I remember well was Albert Leggott from Owston Ferry. He was a salvage man, a real expert, and if a keel or a barge sank, you could bet your life Albert would be given the job of going and lifting it. He had two sons, Billy and Tommy, and each had a boat: Billy's was wooden, but Tommy's was a steel sloop, which could move really quickly. Eventually, Billy gave up the river life, but Tommy made a good career out of it. He decided that sail was too slow and had an engine put in his boat, which was called the *Salvage.* As things got busier, he asked me if I would like to skipper it for him. As I was just newly married I had to refuse, as it would have meant I could only go home at the weekends, which wouldn't have gone down very well with my new wife!

5.

Towards the 'Nineties'

The United Towing Company of Hull continued to work assisting ships which met with various accidents and mishaps on their way along the rivers.

9. The *Fort Fraser* ran aground at Paull on 12th September 1946.

One of these was the *Fort Fraser*, a steamer of 7,134 tons, carrying a cargo of 2,800 standards of timber from Sweden. She ran ashore early in the morning of 12th September 1946 while navigating through one of the dense fogs common on the river, and the tugs *Irishman* and *Krooman* had to go to her assistance. She was, however, clear of the Humber traffic lanes, and was therefore in no danger. It was even reported that her crew was passing the time sunbathing on her decks! She could not be refloated until high tide that evening.

In June 1946 a tanker came to Hull – the first German ship to arrive there after the war. She was called the *Mittel Meer*, and carried a cargo of sugar beet and molasses. A British crew replaced the Germans on board, and took over the vessel which was in very good nick.

In 1947, there was a very hard winter, and at the end of February came a sudden thaw. The river banks simply couldn't cope with the rise in water levels, and at Morton, just on the northern edge of Gainsborough, they burst altogether. Hundreds of acres of land were flooded, and in the low lying areas, people were forced to live in their bedrooms since their ground floors were under water.

As a direct result of that disaster, two floating derricks from Holland were hired to take part in the giant operation needed to strengthen the banks. My father piloted them up to Morton itself, as at that time he was the only pilot who was qualified to navigate past Keadby Bridge.

The Trent River Board ordered thousands of tons of slag to be dropped into the river starting at about twenty yards from the bank. This method was used to encourage the silt to settle between the slag and the bank, and the levels were built up gradually until the correct height was reached. The slag was brought from Gunness, some twelve miles to the north, close to Keadby bridge, where it was loaded. It was then dumped wherever it was needed to bolster weak points in the banks. I would estimate that the present day banks are in fact as much as five or six feet higher than they were then, and should be much safer as a result.

On December 2nd of that same year, a ship called the *Graveller* was towing three barges loaded with gravel when the crew decided to anchor up for the night because of fog closing in. While they were turning round to face the tide, the second barge in tow, the *Trent 10*, ran into the first one, holing herself

10. Above: One of the Dutch pontoon cranes passing under the raised Keadby bridge on April 15th 1947.

11. The same crane being towed in open water along the Trent towards Morton.

in the process. She sank rapidly, and the *Graveller*, in attempting to come to her rescue, ran herself aground on the bows and deck of the now almost submerged barge.

They sounded the siren and called for help. They were heard by a signalman on duty at Hull East Railway who raised the alarm. A pilot launch was sent to the rescue, but it also went aground, so the police built a wooden bridge across the mud to the stranded tug and helped the crew ashore. As I said earlier, the Humber could be a very dangerous river in bad weather.

During the Fifties, everyone was employed if they wanted to be. Scunthorpe was nicknamed 'The town of the fivers', because things were going so well, and I used to wonder what on earth they found to do with all the steel we produced. This was the best time of our working lives and a period of prosperity never to be repeated.

The Humber ferry ran from New Holland to Hull, and provided a good service, usually taking about twenty minutes. At low tide it took much longer, of course, because of the sand banks. Ships had been known to run aground, so they had to wait for the tide to change.

The vessels I remember were all named after famous castles: the *Tattershall*, the *Wingfield* (in Suffolk) and the *Lincoln*. I have travelled on these paddle steamers many times, and it saved a lot of time as otherwise the nearest crossing was at Keadby, where the King George V Bridge is situated, a detour of twenty-five extra miles.

This bridge was sealed during the sixties, never to lift again, as a result of which sloops and keels could no longer operate, given the mere thirty feet of clearance available there. There have also been one or two incidents where a ship broke its mooring and ran into the bridge. This meant it was obliged to stay there until the tide changed, and both the bridge and wheelhouse suffered a good deal of damage.

The port of Hull at the entrance to the river Humber was once one of the largest fishing ports in the country. In the late seventies there was trouble with Iceland over fishing rights—known as the 'Cod War'—and, once they got a two hundred mile limit, most of the Hull trawlers were put out of operation and were sold, converted, or just broken up. This saw the end of yet another flourishing industry on the river, with hundreds of people laid off work. The King George Dock seems to be the main dock still in business today, but fish is not landed in anything like the quantities it once was.

Immingham Docks were very busy; they could handle up to 25,000 ton ships, and also repair conventional submarines. All kinds of materials are handled here, and ships can operate during high or low tides.

Those who travelled the rivers regularly knew the special names given to various sections along their length. Going from Burton Stather, one would encounter places such as: Hillside, the Amcott Hook, Neap House, Keadby roads, the bridge, and the bends in the river, commonly known as 'bights'. Whenever we got together, people always seemed to talk about happenings on the river, and we all knew just where any given incident had taken place as soon as they mentioned the local name.

In the early 'eighties', a new bridge was opened at Althorpe, neatly diverting almost all of the traffic normally making use of Keadby Bridge, which had become a time-consuming bottleneck.

About nine months after the opening of this bridge came the moment when they opened the longest suspension bridge in the world, the Humber Bridge. This linked Barton to Hessle, and has been immensely helpful to everyone living and working around the Grimsby area.

There are viewing areas situated at each end of the bridge, and it attracts thousands of visitors.

Of course, not everyone benefits from progress, and the paddle steamers were put out of business immediately. Two of the ships went south, while the *Lincoln Castle* moored alongside the bridge and opened as a restaurant. However this venture didn't work out and she was eventually sold to work in Grimsby*.

The river has still continued to have its incidents, such as the tragedy of the helicopter which hit the mast of a German ship while attempting to photograph the Humber. It plunged straight into the water and two cameramen were drowned.

In 1988 a coaster loaded with bricks ran into a dredger and sank right in the middle of the channel. It had to be moved, of course, but there was a great deal of trouble in the doing of it. The crane which was set up to help in this operation toppled over, although, fortunately no-one was injured. They had to cut the ship in half in the finish, and take it to New Holland in two pieces.

These, then, are some of the experiences of a life spent almost entirely in the same little corner of the world, and of my acquaintance with two rivers as a man and a boy. I have written them down because they represent a way of life that has gone forever, except in the minds and hearts of those like myself for whom they will always form a most treasured memory.

---

* At the time of publishing this brief look at *Life on the Trent and Humber Rivers* the *Lincoln Castle* lies adjacent to the newly opened National Heritage Fishing Centre by the Alexandra Dock in Grimsby where she is again used as a 'pub' and licensed restaurant.